# THE SCHOOLKIDS' JOKE BOOK TOO!

*Also compiled by Brough Girling*

The Schoolkids' Joke Book

# THE SCHOOLKIDS' JOKE BOOK TOO!

**COMPILED BY**
**BROUGH GIRLING**

**ILLUSTRATED BY**
**TONY BLUNDELL**

Collins
*An imprint of HarperCollinsPublishers*

First published in Great Britain by CollinsChildren'sBooks in 1998

3 5 7 9 8 6 4 2

CollinsChildren'sBooks is a division of
HarperCollins*Publishers* Ltd,
77-85 Fulham Palace Road,
Hammersmith, London W6 8JB

ISBN 0 00 694585 6

Printed and bound in Great Britain by
Caledonian International Book Manufacturing Ltd,
Glasgow G64

Introducing... by unpopular demand...

# THE SCHOOLKIDS' JOKE BOOK TOO!!

Following the megajoketastic success of THE SCHOOLKIDS' JOKE BOOK, this new book contains zillions of classroom fresh side-splitters, all collected from the street-cred, worldly-wise, baseball-caps-on-backwards inhabitants of the schools listed at the back of the book!

Some of these jokes are so new they've still got dew on them. Some are so old they were ancient when your mum was still a Brownie!

Amazingly, the joke most sent in by schoolkids was: 'What did the big chimney say to the little chimney? *You're too young to smoke*,' and that's *so* old that I haven't put it in the book (except in this bit).

The **STAR JOKES** are ones I really like because I've hardly ever heard them before!

**Brough Girling**

# DAFT DADS

Father: How many times have I told you to stop playing with that calculator?
Son: Er... 343,128.2!
**Steven Green**

Boy: Have you heard of the idiot who keeps saying no?
Dad: No.
**Simon Warner**

Boy: Dad, you've got holes in your trousers
Dad: No I haven't!
Boy: Well how did you get your legs in them, then?!
**Faiza Ahmad**

When my mum and dad got engaged she asked him if he would be giving her a ring. He said, 'Yes, of course. What's your number?'
**Jenny Lacock**

What did the daft dad do when he got a wasp in his ear?
*He shot it*!
**Andrew Beales**

My dad puts straw on his rhubarb, but I prefer custard on mine!
**Kieran McKenzie**

What will you do when you're as big as your dad?
*Go on a diet*!
**Rebecca Bartlett**

My dad's burnt his ear really badly.
How did he do that?
*He was ironing
and the phone rang*!
**Stuart Baird**

What do you grow in your garden, Dad?
*Tired*!
**Helen Dyer**

My Dad is built upside down
What do you mean?
*His feet smell and his nose runs*!
**Christopher Norton**

Boy: Dad, where's the English channel?
Dad: *I don't know, our TV doesn't pick it up...*
**Philip Bartlett**

# FUNNY FAVOURITES

What is a bird's favourite computer game?
*Tweet Fighter*!
**Philip Lickley**

What's a skunk's favourite entertainment?
*Watching smellivision*!
**Daniel Walters**

What's a hairdresser's favourite dog?
*A shampoodle*!
**Dean Walters**

What's a sea monster's favourite food?
*Fish and ships*!
**Bernadette McDonald**

What's a monster's
favourite board
game?
*Monstopoly*!
**Nick Simmons**

What's an Australian animal's favourite computer game?
*Mortal Wombat*!
**Philip Lickley**

What's a ghost's favourite ride at the fair?
*The scary-go-round, or the roller-ghoster*!
**Hayley Clibbery**

Where's a shark's favourite holiday destination?
*Finland*!
**Liam Taylor**

What's a plumber's favourite vegetable?
*A leek*!
**Jonny Bishop**

What's a parrot's
favourite food?
*Pollyfilla*!
**Hayley Potter**

What's Dracula's
favourite pet?
*A bloodhound*!
**Danny Hammett**

What's a skeleton's
favourite musical
instrument?
*A Trombone*!
**Josh Johnson**

What's a hedgehog's
favourite food?
*Prickled onions*!
**Ashlie Graham**

What's an elephant's
favourite game?
*Squash*!
**Stuart Adamson**

What's a ghost's favourite breakfast cereal?
*Dreaded wheat*!
**Hayley Hughes**

What do you call a budgie run over by a lawn mower?
*Shredded Tweet*!
**Arron Creaney**

What's a stone's favourite music?
*Rock and roll*!
**Allan Yates**

What's a ghost's favourite food?
*Spookgetti*!
**Adam McClement**
[Editor: Sorry, Adam, I thought it was *Ghoulash*!]

What's a cat's favourite food?
*Mice pudding*!
**Chris Hampton**

What's a polar bear's favourite food?
*Iceburgers*!
**Lisa Glabham**

What's a rabbit's favourite sweet?
*A lollihop*!
**Kyle McRoberts**

What's a spaceman's favourite game?
*Astronauts and crosses*!
**Joseph Nelson**

What's a crocodile's favourite game?
*Swallow my leader*!
**Gary Boyd**

What's an alligator's favourite game?
*Snap*!
**Stuart Adamson**

# DOTTY DOCTORS

Doctor, Doctor, I think I'm turning into a bridge.
*Really, what's come over you?*
So far, a car and two buses!
**Robert Crawshaw**

Doctor, Doctor, I think I'm turning into an orange.
*It's OK, you've just been playing too much squash!*
**Samantha Millar**

Incidentally, why did the orange go to the doctor?
*He wasn't peeling very well!*
**Donna Shiels**

Doctor, Doctor, a cockroach bit me.
*Don't worry, it's just a nasty bug that's going around!*
**Damon Doherty**

Doctor, Doctor, my nose is running.
*Well why don't you run after it?!*
**Toby Marshall**

Doctor, Doctor, I've swallowed a mouth organ and it keeps playing tunes in my tummy.
*Well, it's lucky you didn't swallow a piano!*
**Emily Blake**

Doctor, Doctor I think I'm turning into a piglet.
How long have you felt like this?
*About a weeeeeek!*
**Catherine Tucker**

A man went to the doctor, and the doctor said, 'Did you drink your medicine after your bath, like I told you to?'
'No,' *said the man, 'by the time I'd drunk the bath, I couldn't manage the medicine*!'
**Andrew Evans**

Doctor, Doctor I think I'm getting smaller.
*Well you'll just have to be a little patient!*
**Arran Grimes**

Doctor, Doctor, I think I need glasses.
*You certainly do, this is a fish and chip shop!*
**Gareth Robinson**

Docto, Doctor, I keep thinking I'm a bird
*Well perch over there and I'll tweet you in a minute*!
**Andrew Page**

Doctor, Doctor, my son has swallowed a bullet
*Well don't point him at me*!
**Marcus Cridland**

Doctor, Doctor, I've swallowed a roll of film
*Don't worry, nothing serious will develop!*
**Jaime Norman**

Doctor, Doctor I've only got 59 seconds to live!
*I'll see you in a minute.*
**Nicholas Wright**

What happened to the plastic surgeon who stood too close to the fire?
*He melted*!
**Jaime Norman**

# RIOTOUS RIDDLES

Where do policemen live?
*999 Letsby Avenue*!
**Steven Green**

What can you make that you can't see?
*Noise*!
**Andrew Simpson**

Where do aliens go
to study?
*Mooniversity*!
**Jay Parker**

What is Santa's
phone number?
*O,O,O*!
**Mohamed Ellaboudy**

What do snowmen do in cold weather?
*Sit round a candle*.
What do snowmen do in very cold weather?
*Light it*!
**Sam Ryman**

What's purple and thousands of miles long?
*The grape wall of China!*
**Kevin Soopen**

How did the ghost get back into his coffin?
*He used a skeleton key!*
**Adam Tirlon**

What's pink and turns blue?
*A swimmer in winter!*
**Martin Podmore**

Why do nuns walk on their heels?
*To save their souls*!
**Charlene Cooper**

How do you make gold soup?
*Put twenty-five carrots in it*!
**Leopold Wallo**

What's the difference between a fireman and
a soldier?
*You can't dip a fireman
in your egg*!
**Phillip Henson**

What's short and
green and
goes camping?
*A boy sprout*!
**Josh Simpson**

How do ducks
play tennis?
*With tennis
quackets*!
**Lawrence Gower**

Who has a sack and likes to bite people?
*Santa Jaws*!
**Chris Braken**

What goes up and down but never moves?
*Stairs*!
**Maryam Butt**

What happened to the man who couldn't tell the difference between putty and porridge?
*His teeth stuck together and his windows fell out*!
**Craig Coyles**

What did the musician take to the supermarket?
*A Chopin Liszt*!
**Kevin Soopen**

Which old pop group kills germs?
*The Bleach Boys*!
**Steven Perry**

Why do wizards drink so much tea?
*Sorcerers need cuppas*!
**James Smith**

Why did
the mushroom
go to the disco?
*Because he's a
fun-guy*!
**Martin Skingley**

What's the cheapest
way to hire a car?
*Put bricks under
the wheels*!
**Crispin Northey**

What do jelly babies
wear on their feet?
*Gum boots*!
**Samantha Rutherford**

What's the
difference between
someone desperate
to go to the toilet, and
someone very, very ill?
*One is dying to go, the other is going to die*!
**Holly Puckett**

Why shouldn't you play cards in a jungle?
*There are too many cheetahs*!
**Vikki Marie Tyler**

Why did the chewing gum cross the road?
*Because it was stuck to the chicken's foot!*
**James Smith** [also **Adam Howard**]

Can the orange box?
*No, but the baked bean can!*
**Ervin Falic**

Why did the Ancient Egyptian girl start crying?
*Her daddy had just become a mummy!*
**Terri Hughes**

What goes 'oom, oom'?
*A cow walking backwards!*
**Jemma Allcock**

What is the world's brainiest mountain?
*Mount Cleverest!*
**Oscar Bishop**

What's the tastiest planet in the solar system?
*Mars!*
**Gary Bridgeman**

How do you cook sausages in a jungle?
*Under a gorilla*!
**Fred Cooper**

Where is the best country to cook chips?
*Greece*!
**Adam Tirlon**

Why do the Spice Girls only work at weekends?
*It takes them all week to relearn their words*!
**Alison Stanley**

Why do headteachers never look out of the window in the morning?
*They wouldn't have anything to do in the afternoons*!
**Joanna Rigg**

What two words have the most letters in them?
*Post box*!
**Helena Hamilton**

What does an old bird do at the Post Office every week?
*P-p-p-p-pick up a pension*!
**Brian Sheehy**

Why did they give the postman the sack?
*To put his letters in*!
**Steven Green**

STAR JOKE * STAR JOKE * STAR JOKE

How did they divide the Roman Empire?
*With a pair of caesars*!
**Emma Bunting**

# YUKKY JOKES

Things to say to a dinner lady:
'*Excuse me, are these sesame seeds or have you just sneezed?*'
**Kyle Harper**

What's big and grey and has underarm problems?
*A Smellyphant*!
**Philippa Chapman Pincher**

A little boy asked his teacher if he could go to the toilet.
'Only if you can recite the alphabet,' said the teacher.
'*OK,*' *said the boy.* '*ABCDEFGHIJKLMNOQ RSTUVWXYZ.*'
'Where's the P?' said the teacher
'*Halfway down my leg,*' *said the boy*!
**Hannah Kirkpatrick**

What's green and white and swings through the trees?
*Tarzan's hankie*!
**Adam Chapman**

How do nits go on holiday?
*British Hairways*!
**Stuart Adamson**

Mum, Can I have a puppy for Christmas?
*No, you'll have turkey like everyone else*!
**Michael Jamison**

Knock! Knock!
*Who's there*?
Stan
*Stan who*?
Stan back I'm going to be sick!
**Philippa Chapman Pincher**

What's green and turns red at the flick of a switch?
*I don't know.*
A frog in a liquidiser
*Yuk! That's sick!*
So was my mum when she saw the liquidiser!
**Matthew Girling**

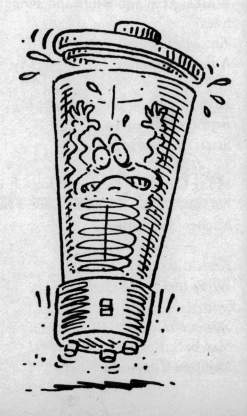

# NUTTY NEWS

A large hole has appeared in Oxford Street.
*Police are looking into it.*
**Gabriella Wheeler**

A cow has been seen walking along a road.
*It turned into a field.*
**Emma McConville**

A sandwich walked into a pub today and ordered a drink.
*He was told by the barman that they didn't serve food.*
**Andrew Jenkinson**

# STAR JOKE * STAR JOKE * STAR JOKE

A chameleon had a heart attack today.
*It was trying to cross a tartan rug.*
**Carolyn Hall**

Two men broke into a shoe shop today and took some shoes.
*It's thought they were a pair of sneakers.*
**Cara Fullerton**

A man has been found guilty of stealing a calendar.
*He got twelve months.*
**Aston Wiggans**

A woman went into a shop today and asked if she could try on a dress in the window.
*The manager suggested that it might be better to use a changing room.*
**Polly Nicholson**

Announcement: 'The train arriving at platforms 6, 7 & 8 is coming in sideways...'
**Shauni MacGregor**

This morning a chicken jumped off a bridge into a river.
*Police think it was fed up with jokes about crossing the road.*
**Matthew Curry**

There was a tragedy in Ireland today.
*A man did the river dance, and drowned.*
**Adam Chapman**

Britain's latest boxing champion is a featherweight.

*He tickles his opponents to death...*

**Grant Norgrove**

Tragedy struck a paper boy early this morning.

*He blew away...*

**Kyle Suter**

A man went into a barber's shop this morning and said, 'How much is a haircut?'
*'Four pounds,' said the barber.*
'How much is a shave?' asked the man.
*'Two pounds,' said the barber.*
'OK,' said the man, 'shave my head!'
**Maryam Butt**

A man has been caught climbing on the roof of a pub.
*He'd been told that the drinks were on the house.*
**Michael Nutt**

## STAR JOKE * STAR JOKE * STAR JOKE

This morning two televisions got married.
*The wedding was terrible, but the reception was great!*
**Emma Humphry**

There was confusion at a bank today. A man rushed in and pointed his finger at one of the staff.
*'This is a muck-up,' he said.*
'Don't you mean a hold-up?' said the cashier.
*'No. it's a muck-up, I've forgotten my gun!'*
**Adam Chapman.**

A musical thief struck today.
*He got away with the lute.*
**Paul Francis**

A boy was asked today if he had had help with his homework.
*'No,' he replied. 'I got it wrong all by myself.'*
**Rebecca Bartlett**

Today there was a race between a tap, a dog and a tomato.
*The tap was running, then the dog took the lead, and the tomato couldn't ketchup.*
**Christopher Chalker**

A motorist was stopped by the police for driving, in reverse, up the motorway.
*When they asked him why he was doing it, he said it was because he knew the rules of the road backwards.*
**Jonny Bishop**

# WHAT DID THEY SAY?

What did the candle say to the other candle?
*Do you want to go out tonight?*
**Sarah Dunn**

What did the biscuit say when his brother was run over?
*Oh crumbs!*
**Charlene Cooper**

## STAR JOKE * STAR JOKE * STAR JOKE

What did the sad plumber say to his girlfriend?
*It's all over Flo!*
**Ryan Bradford**

What did the schoolboy say when he sat down to eat his school dinner?
*'Through the teeth*
*And past the gums,*
*Look out stomach*
*Here it comes!*
**Natalie Gardner**

What did the skeleton say when he went into the restaurant?
*Have you got any spare ribs*!
**Siân Dunlop**

What did the dog say when it sat on some sandpaper?
*Ruff*!
**Jonny Bishop**

What did the kangaroo say on New Year's Eve?
*Hoppy New Year*!
**Elizabeth Tilley**

What does Santa say when he's gardening?
*Hoe, Hoe, Hoe*!
**Helena Hamilton**

What did ET's mum say when he finally got home?
*Where on earth have you been*?
**Curtis Headley**

## STAR JOKE * STAR JOKE * STAR JOKE

What did the vampire say to his victim?
*Your neck's on my list*!
**Stephen Wilkes**

What did one eye say to the other eye?
*Between you and me, something smells.*
**Rebecca Wood**

What did the balloon say to the pin?
*Hi, buster!*
**Hannah Stadford**

What did the hat say to the scarf?
*You hang around and I'll go on ahead!*
**Wallis Murphy**

What did the bull say when he came back from
the china shop?
*I've had a really smashing time!*
**Oliver Barker**

What did the man say
when he walked into a bar?
*OUCH*! (It was an iron bar)
**David Walker**

What did Cinderella say to the photographer?
*Some day my prints will come.*
**Leopold Wallo**

What did the big telephone say to the small
telephone?
*You're too young to be engaged*!
**Catherine Morrison**

What did the wall say to the other wall?
*Meet me at the corner*!

What did the baby hedgehog say to the cactus?
*Hello, Mum*!
**Bernadette McDonald**

What did the ghost say when it came home after
a night's haunting?
*I'm dead on my feet*!
**Liam Taylor**

What did the children say to the snowman on his
birthday?
*'Freeze a jolly good fellow*!'
**Jane Custer**

# BARMY BOOKS!

*The Earthquake* by Major Disaster
*Breakfast is Ready* by Chris P Bacon
*The Haunted House* by Hugo First
*The Broken Window* by E Didit
*Electric Faults* by Lou Swires
**All from Stuart Adamson**

*Spooked Out* by Terry Fied
*Road Safety* by Luke Left & Den Right
**William Boothroyd**

*Springtime* by Teresa Green
*On the Beach* by C Shaw
*The Post Script* by Adeline Extra
*Long Hot Summer* by I Scream
*Swimming the Channel* by Frances Near
*Jungle Fever*
by Amos Quito

*At the North Pole* by I C Blast
*Stranded on the Motorway* by Buster Tyre
*Making Waterproof Clothes* by Anne O'Rack
*Pig Breeding* by Lena Bacon
**All from children at Wycliffe Middle School**

*How to Feed Dogs* by Nora Bone
**Kate Roper**

*Famous Pirates* by R Jimlad
*Daft Jokes* by M T Head
*Get Rich Quick* by Robin Banks
**Alison Edgar**

# RIDICULOUS RIDDLES

What kind of glasses do ghosts wear?
*Spooktackles*!
**Naomi Carpenter**

Where do spooks buy stamps?
*The Ghost Office*!
**Stephen Wilkes**

What do idiots say?
*I don't know.*
**Rebecca Davies**

How do ghosts like their breakfast eggs?
*Terrifried*!
**Alex Morgan**

What runs round a field but doesn't move?
*A fence*!
**Sam Bizzell**

What's red and wobbles and hovers in the air?
*A jellycopter*!
**Kate Roper**

What crisps can fly?
*Plain*!
**Aston Wiggans**

What happened when the bell fell in the water?
*It got wringing wet*!
**Amy Millichope**

What's red on the outside, grey on the inside, and very crowded?
*A bus full of elephants*!
**David Evans**

Why do elephants paint the bottom of their feet yellow?
*So they can hide upside down in a bowl of custard.*
But I've never seen an elephant upside down in a bowl of custard.
*There you are. It works*!
**Rebecca Davies**

What's the difference between a rabbit and a gorilla?
*A rabbit doesn't look like a gorilla*!
**Samuel Johnson**

What flowers grow between your chin and your nose?
*Tulips*!
**Saninder Virdee**

What does the Queen drink?
*Royalty*! (royal tea – gettit?)
**Sam Bizzell**
[Editor: No, Sam, I get the Beano]

How many teachers does it take to work the school photocopier?
*Who cares, so long as it keeps them out of our classroom*!
**Emma Morris**

How do you confuse a naughty Inuit child?
*Tell him to stand in the corner of the igloo*!
**Simon Shaw**

Why are ghosts bad at lying?
*You can see right through them*!
**Jacqueline Alexander**

What's green and white and hops?
*A frog sandwich*!
**Kate Roper**

How do you count cows?
*On a cowculator*!
**Stuart Adamson**
[Editor: Sorry, Stuart, I thought you count all the legs and then divide by four!]

What does a cat wash its mouth with?
*Mouse wash*!
**Luke Folgate**

## STAR JOKE * STAR JOKE * STAR JOKE

What musical instrument did they play in the olden days?
*The Anglosaxaphone*!
**Samuel Johnson**

Why did the one-eyed man give up teaching?
*What's the point with only one pupil*!
**Natasha Blackwell**

What vegetable has the sweetest rhythm?
*Sugar beet*!
**Rebecca Hutchinson**

What do you call a rich rabbit?
*A millionhare*!
**Adam Hunter**

What's grey and has a trunk?
*A mouse going on holiday*!
**Catherine Morrison**

Where do baby apes sleep?
*In apricots*!
**Stuart Adamson**

Why did the boy dress up his front teeth?
*The dentist said he was going to take them out*!
**Hazel Dunlop**

# WHAT DO YOU GET?

What do you get if you cross a cow with a letterbox?
*A postman pat*!
**Christopher Norton**

What do you get if you cross a centipede with a parrot?
*A walkie-talkie*!
**Saninder Virdee**

# STAR JOKE * STAR JOKE * STAR JOKE

What do you get if you put up too many Christmas decorations?
*Tinselitis*!
**Ross Preston**

What do you get if you cross the Arctic with a vampire?
*Frostbite*!
**Owen Demonick**

What do you get if you're being chased by a very angry shark?
*As far away as possible!*
**Rhiannon Somerset**

What do you get if you leave a pile of bones in the sun?
*A skele-tan!*
**Danny Hammett**

What do you get if you cross an Oxo cube with a hyena?
*A laughing stock!*
**James Elder**

What do you get if you cross a giraffe with a hedgehog?
*A hair brush with a very long handle.*
**Kyle Haworth**

What do you get if you wash your front door step?
*A broken washing machine*!
**Kerri Jones**

What do you get if you drop a piano down a mine shaft?
*A flat minor*!
**Jonathan Overton**

What do you get if you cross the Atlantic ocean with the Titanic?
*About half way*!
**Josh Johnson**

What do you get if a cat sits on a beach at Christmas?
*Sandy claws*!
**Joanna Bates**

What do you get if you cross a vampire and a computer?
*Love at first byte*!
**Kimberley Taylor**

What do you get someone for their birthday if they've already got everything?
*A burglar alarm*!
**Claire Lyford**

What do you get if you cross a rooster, a French dog and a large Australian animal?
*A cock-apoodle-Roo!*
**Megs Louise Philp**

Where do giraffes keep their money?
*In the top branches!*
**Naomi Carpenter**

What do you get if you cross an elephant with a sparrow?
*Broken telephone lines*!
**Rhiannon William**

What do you get if you pour boiling water down a rabbit hole?
*Hot cross bunnies*!
**William Holloway**

What do you get when a pig gets fleas?
*Pork Scratchings*!
**Philippa Chapman Pincher**

What do you get if you cross a dog with a jelly?
*Colliewobbles*!
Henry Posner

## STAR JOKE * STAR JOKE * STAR JOKE

What do you get if you cross a pig with a dinosaur?
*Jurassic pork*!
Leon Murray

What do you get if you cross a rabbit with a flea?
*A bugs bunny*!
Leane Falls

What do you get if you cross a cow, a kangeroo and a camel?
*Lumpy milkshakes*!
Emily Gailey

What do you get if you cross a dog with a telephone?
*A golden receiver*!
**Ryan Bradford**

# FUNNY FOOTY

Which Manchester United player is always laughing?
*Ryan Giggles!*
**Ryan McCann**

Why do goalkeepers have baths before they go to bed?
*To keep clean sheets!*
**Andrew Pamflett**

Why won't midfield players travel by aeroplane?
*In case they are put on the wing*!
**Andrew Pamflett**

Why do Liverpool need lights?
*They've lost all their matches*!
**Joshua Edwards**

Why did the ref send off all the chickens in a football team?
*There were too many fowls*!
**Hazel Quinn**

Defender: Why didn't you stop that ball?
*Goalie: I thought that was what the net was for*!
**David Bower**

## STAR JOKE * STAR JOKE * STAR JOKE

How do you spy on a bad football manager?
*Through a hole in defence*!
**Mark Thackray**

Why can't cars play football?
*They've only got one boot*!
**Steven Scott**

Which team do snakes play for?
*Slitherpool*!
**Thomas Walsh**

Why is Cinderella so bad at playing football?
*Because she runs away from the ball*!
**Thomas Walsh**
[Editor: I thought it was because she had a pumpkin for a coach!]

Who is the most important player in a ghosts' football team?
*The ghoulkeeper*!
**Natasha Bekshi**

Which two players in the Liverpool team have four first names?
*Michael Thomas and David James*!
**Ryan McCann**

What's the difference between the England football team and wet paint?
*It's more enjoyable to watch the wet paint dry*!
**Áine McKerr** (from Ireland!)

Why did the manager have the football pitch flooded?
*So he could bring on his sub*!
**Lawrence Gower**

Where do spiders play football?
*Webley*!
**David Small**

How do footballers keep cool?
*They stand by a fan*!
**Kimberley Taylor**

What do bad goalkeepers and Dracula have in common?
*They both hate crosses*!
**Andrew Pamflett**

What happens if you cross a football team with an ice cream?
*You get Aston Vanilla*!
**Julie Wilson**
[Editor: or they always get licked!]

# KNUTTY KNOCK! KNOCKS!

Knock! Knock!
*Who's there?*
Mustard Bean
*Mustard Bean who?*
You Mustard Bean a big disappointment to your parents. They probably expected a boy or a girl!
**Philip Morrison**

Knock! Knock!
*Who's there?*
Lettuce
*Lettuce who?*
Lettuce in, it's freezing out here!
**Sharon Ellison**

Knock! Knock!
*Who's there?*
Olive
*Olive who?*
Olive just up the road!
**Jill Stephens**

Knock! Knock!
*Who's there?*
Police!
*Police who?*
Police open this door!
**Natalie Jemmott**

Knock! Knock!
*Who's there?*
Dishwasher
*Dishwasher who?*
Dish washer way I shpoke before I has falsh teef!
**Kirsty Glenton**

Knock! Knock!
*Who's there?*
Irish Stew
*Irish stew who?*
Irish stew in the name of the law!
**Amy Paxton**

Knock! Knock!
*Who's there?*
Egbert
*Egbert who?*
Egbert no bacon!
**Hannah Moore**

Knock! Knock!
*Who's there?*
Tuba
*Tuba who?*
Tuba toothpaste
**Matthew Robin**

Knock! Knock!
*Who's there?*
Doughnut
*Doughnut who?*
Doughnut ask such
silly questions!
**Robert Harewood**

Knock! Knock!
*Who's there?*
Cook
*Cook who?*
You're the first one I've heard this year!
**Stephen Scott**

Knock! Knock!
*Who's there?*
Cornflakes
*Cornflakes who?*
I'll tell you next week – it's a cereal!
**Clare Wilcockson**

Knock! Knock!
*Who's there?*
Interrupting cow
*Interrup—*
MOO MOO MOO!
**Anon**

Knock! Knock!
*Who's there?*
Little old lady
*Little old lady who?*
I didn't know you could yodel!
**Julie Wade**

# CREATURES TO CRACK YOU UP

What's the difference between a buffalo and a bison?
*You can't wash your hands in a buffalo!*
**Natasha Brown**

Where do you find a tortoise with no legs?
*Wherever you put it!*
**Katrina Dixon**

What type of animal do you need when it's cold?
*A little otter!*
**William Tweed**

## STAR JOKE * STAR JOKE * STAR JOKE

Where do dogs go when they lose their tails?
*A retailer!*
**Danny Watkins**

What do sheep wash with?
*Baaars of soap*!
**Alexander Newberry**

Where do cows go on holiday?
*Moo York*!
**Paul Hatton**

Why can't you play jokes on snakes?
*You can't pull their legs*!
**Maryam Butt**

How do sheep keep warm?
*Central bleating*!
**Sophie Nash**

What do you call a wet deer?
*A raindeer*!
**Katrina Dixon**

What are spiders' webs no good for?
*Flies*!
**Alex Paddick**

## STAR JOKE * STAR JOKE * STAR JOKE

Have you heard about the two deer that ran away to get married?
*They anteloped*!
**Rhiannon William**

What bird
plays football?
*A gullkeeper*!
**Thomas Walsh**

How do you stop a mole digging up your lawn?
*Take his spade away!*
**Claire Lyford**

Why did the chicken cross the road?
*To collect her pension.*
Er I don't get it...
*Neither did she – she wasn't old enough!*
**Kate Kay**

Why did the chicken cross the park?
*To get to the other slide!*
**Michael Pullar**

How do chickens dance?
*Chick to chick!*
**Kyle Haworth**

A man had a pet centipede, and he told it to go down to the corner shop and get a newspaper. The man fell asleep, and when he woke up an hour later the centipede was still in the hall, and there was no sign of a newspaper.

'Hey,' said the man. 'I told you to go and get a paper.'

'*Give me a chance,*' said the centipede, '*I'm still putting my shoes on*!'

**Claire Morris**

[Editor: It reminds me of the tortoise that used to go down to the corner shop and come back with last week's newspaper!]

What creature wears a coat in the winter and pants in the summer?

*A dog*!

**Samantha Rutherford**

What bird is always out of breath?
*A puffin*!
**Richard Bellerby**

One snake said to another, 'What's twelve minus three?'
*'I don't know,' said the other, 'I'm an adder*!'
**David Crooks**

Where does a fish keep his money?
*In a riverbank*!
**Dwain Steele**

What do birds of prey use after a bath?
*Falcon Powder*!
**Andrew Page**

Why couldn't the penguin fly?
*He couldn't get out of the wrapper*!
**Kyle Matthews**

Who solves mysteries in the farmyard
*Inspector Horse*!
**Jason Mclean**

What's grey and hovers?
*An elecopter*!
**Ruth Danes**

What lives in Scotland and says, 'Who's a pretty boy?'
*The Loch Ness Budgerigar*!
**Bill North**

Have you heard about the very polite horse?
*He always let his rider go over the jump first*!
**Hayley McKeown**

What fur do you get from a wolf?
*As fur away as possible*!
**Jack Dight**

What's black and white and red all over?
*A blushing zebra*!
**Saninder Virdee**
[Editor: I thought it was a newspaper, or a sun-burnt penguin!]

Where do you take a sick dog?
*The dogtor*!
**Richard Martin**
[Editor: Yes, Richard, and you take a sick horse to a horsepital, and a sick wasp to a waspital!]

Incidentally, what do you give sick ants?
*Antibiotics*!
**Andrew Beales**

What animal has four legs, no sense of humour and flies?
*A dead hyena*!
**Daniel Walters**

What illness do birds get most?
*Flu*!
**Susila Baybars**

# WHAT DO YOU CALL?

What do you call a dirty Teletubby?
*Stinky Winky!*
**Emma Mckay**

What do you call two rows of cabbages?
*A dual cabbageway!*
**Barbara McCartney**

## STAR JOKE * STAR JOKE * STAR JOKE

What do you call an animal that goes 'clip-'?
*A one legged horse!*
**Samantha Rutherford**

Boy: What do you call a green slimy thing with big teeth that slides around looking vicious?
Other boy: *I don't know*
First boy: Neither do I, but one of them has just gone down your collar!
**Andrew Evans**

What do you call people who spy on sheep?
*Shepherd spies*!
**Katherine Hueston**

What do you call a group of men who wander about with bolts through their necks?
*Bolton Wanderers*!
**Thomas Walsh**

What do you call
a man with a seagull
on his head?
*Cliff*!
**Luke Folgate**

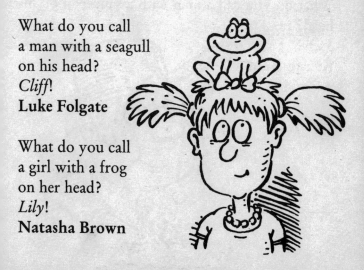

What do you call
a girl with a frog
on her head?
*Lily*!
**Natasha Brown**

What do you call a man with a car number plate on his head?
*Reg!*
**Jane Brown**

What do you call a dead man with a car number plate on his head?
*X Reg!*
**Hannah Fogg**

What do you call a woman who sets fire to her bills?
*Bernadette* (Burn a debt! Geddit!)
**Kate Roper**

What do you call a man with a saucepan on his head?
*Stew!*
**Kieran Reed**

What do you call a skeleton's bike?
*A boneshaker*!
**Thomas Hoskins**

What do you call a woman who sets fire to her bills?
*Bernadette* (Burn a debt! Geddit!)
**Kate Roper**

What do you call
a camel with
three humps?
*Humphrey!*
**Robert Harewood**

What do you call a cold cow?
*A friesian!*
**Jonathan Robinson**

What do you call a crazy spaceman?
*An astronut!*

What do you call a girl with two lavatories?
*Lulu!*
**Amy Muttschall**

What do you call a sheep with no head and no legs?
*A cloud!*
**Ryan Downer**

What do you call something that's red and cheeky?
*Tomato sauce!*
**Steven Parslow**

What do you call a slug in a crash helmet?
*A snail*!
**Aston Wiggans**

What do you call a man who can't stop buying carpets?
*A rug addict*!
**Hamza Darr**

What do you call two chemists?
*A pair of Boots*!
**Crispin Northey**

**STAR JOKE * STAR JOKE * STAR JOKE**

What do you call a famous artist with a cold?
*Van Cough*!
**Mohamed Ellaboudy**

What do you call a girl with eggs and bacon on her head?
*Caff*!
**Jamie O'Connor**

What do you call a potato with high blood pressure?
*A beetroot*!
**Joseph Nelson**

What do you call a detective in bed?
*An undercover agent*!
**Christopher Morse**

What do you call a happy Scottish Mushroom?
*Fungus*!
**Gemma Wilson**

What do you call a gorilla with a machine gun?
*Sir*!
**Adam Gallagher**

What do you call a man sitting on a doorstep?
*Mat*!
**Jonathan Lynch**

What do you call an insect at a sale?
*A jumble bee*!
**Andrew Page**

# STAR JOKE \* STAR JOKE \* STAR JOKE

What do you call a donkey with three legs
*A wonkey*!
**Adam Cooper**

What was Snow White's brother called?
*Egg White*! (Get the yolk?)
**Tom Gibbons**
[Editor: OK, Tom, what's the opposite of white?
*YOLK*!]

What do you call a fish with no eyes?
*FSH*!!!!
**Luke Folgate**

What do you call a polar bear in the Sahara?
*Very lost*!
**Lawrence Gower**

What do you call a man who works in a perfume shop at Christmas?
*Frank-in-scents*!
**Jennifer Webb**

What do you call a man with a car on his head?
*Jack*!
**Adam Gallagher**

# DEAD POSH CLEVER JOKES

Two cats decided to have a race across the English channel.
The French cat was called Un deux trois.
The British cat was called One two three.
*The British cat won because Un deux trois quatre cinq*!!!
**Simon Warner**

Why is six afraid of seven?
*Because seven ate nine*!
**Kate Roper**

If you add 99 to 87, double it and then divide by three, what do you get?
*Probably the wrong answer*!
**Rebecca Bartlett**

When do 2 and 2 make more than 4?
*When they make 22!*
**Ervin Falic**

When are skipping ropes like schoolkids?
*When they're 'taut'!*
**Grant Norgrove**

Father: Sarah, go next door and see how old Mrs Crabapple is.
Sarah: OK
Later...
Sarah: *Dad, Mrs Crabapple is very annoyed and says it's none of your business how old she is*!
**Matthew Edwards**

Where do you find giant snails?
*At the end of giant's fingers!*
**Saninder Virdee**

Why were The Middle Ages often called the Dark Ages?
*Because there were so many 'knights'!*
**Naomi Carpenter**

First child: Where does your mum come from?
Second child: Alaska.
First child: *Oh don't bother, I'll ask her myself!*
**Kirsty Glenton**

Which is correct: 'egg yolks is white,' or 'egg yolk are white?'
*Neither, egg yolks are yellow!*
**Andrea Thompson**

# WHAT DO YOU DO?

What do you do if you find a baby in a cradle on the moon?
*Rocket*!
**Paul Francis**

What do you do if you see a spaceman?
*Park in it, man*!
**Becky Chapman Pincher**
[Editor: So if you see the milkman, put it on your cornflakes man!]

What do you do if you want to see flying saucers?
*Trip up a waiter*!
**Jonny Bishop**

What do you do if you want to make a witch scratch herself?
*Take away her W*!
**Stephen England**

How do you get a ghost to lie down flat?
*Use a spirit level*!
**Helen Dyer**

What do you do if an elephant breaks its toe?
*Call a tow truck*!
**Alison Smyth**

What do you do if you've got a sick frog?
*Give it a hoperation*!
**Emily Gailey**

# POTTY POEM

Our wee school is a great wee school,
It's made of bricks and plaster.
What we don't like in our great wee school
Is the nasty bald headmaster!
He goes to the pub on Saturday night
And he goes to church on Sundays.
He prays to God to give him the strength
To murder us all on Mondays!
**Mathew Saunders**

# TALL STORIES

There were two cows standing in a field. One said to the other, 'What do you think about mad cow disease?'

The other one replied, 'I don't know, I'm a tractor!'
**Hannah Evans**

A piece of string went into a bar and ordered a drink. 'I'm sorry,' said the barman, 'we don't serve pieces of string.'

Another piece of string went into the bar and ordered a drink, and again the barman said, 'Look,

I'm sorry, we don't serve pieces of string.'

A third piece of string went into the bar, and the barman got really cross. 'I've already told your friends that we don't serve pieces of string, and you're a piece of string aren't you?'

'No' said the third piece of string. 'I'm afraid knot!' [a frayed knot, geddit?]
**Joe Brina**

## STAR JOKE * STAR JOKE * STAR JOKE

A man started work in the reception of a hotel. The manager told him to greet guests by their names. 'How will I know what their names are?' asked the man. 'From the labels on their suitcases,' said the manager.

When the first guests arrived the man said, 'Good morning, Mr and Mrs Real Leather.'
**Santosh Joshi**

A man arrived at the gates of heaven and was greeted by St Peter. The man said to the great saint, 'Aren't you bored with standing at these gates for all these centuries letting people in?'

St Peter replied, 'You must remember that in heaven things are different, a million years is but a minute, a million pounds is but five pence.'

'Could you lend me five pence?' said the man quickly.

'Of course,' said St Peter. 'In a minute...'
**David Scott**

A man was released from prison. He went down the road shouting 'I'm free! I'm free! I'm free!'

A small boy heard him, and shouted back, 'I'm four, I'm four, I'm four!'
**Kevin Sooper**

A man went into a shop and said he wanted to buy some pyjamas for the summer.

The shop assistant took out a tape measure and said, 'How long do you want them?'

'From about March to September,' said the man.
**Simon Warner**

A skyscraper was on fire, and a woman looked out of a top window screaming, 'Help Help! My baby is here, help me save her.'

Down in the street below there was a goalkeeper who shouted back. 'Don't worry, I've only let in two goals this season. If you drop the baby out the window, I'll catch it!'

The woman dropped the baby out of the window, and with no difficulty the man caught it. The crowd all cheered. Then he bounced the baby three times and kicked it up the high street!
**Adam Gallagher**

A policeman stopped a woman who was driving the wrong way down a one way street. She apologised and said she was in a hurry. 'I'm so late,' she said, 'look – everyone else is coming back!'
**Michael Heighway**
[Editor: I thought she might have pointed out that she was only going one way!]

Two men where standing on the top of a cliff. One had a budgerigar on each shoulder, and the other had a parrot in one hand and a gun in the other. They both jumped off the cliff and landed on the rocks below. They were badly injured.

The first one spoke: 'I don't think much of this budgie jumping!'

'No,' said the other, 'and I don't think much of this free-fall parrot shooting either!'
**Simon Stich.**

# WHY OH WHY?

Why is tennis such a noisy game?
*Because everyone raises a racket!*
**Matthew Millard**

Why do mice eat candles?
*For light refreshment!*
**Luke Trevon**

Why did the penguin blush?
*Because it saw the polar bear.*
**Simon Warner**

Why did the skeleton cross the road?
*To get to the Body Shop*!
**Charlene Cooper**

Why did the orange stop running down the road?
*It ran out of juice*!
**Balbir Singh**

Why do witches ride on broomsticks?
*Vacuum cleaners are too heavy*!
**Leanne Stephens**

Why didn't the skeleton go to the disco?
*He had no body to go with*!
**Lloyd Dixon**

Why didn't the Egyptians build pyramids in the fog?
*They couldn't see the point*!
**Kevin Soopen**

Why are sheep like ink?
*You put them in pens*!
**Josh Simson**

Why didn't the policeman arrest the man going
the wrong way up a one way street?
*He was walking*!
**Alexander Sloan**

Why did Mickey Mouse go into space?
*He wanted to find Pluto*!
**Natalie Donna Long**

Why did the boy take a pencil and paper upstair
when he went to bed?
*He wanted to draw the curtains*!
**Maryam Butt**

Why are giraffes' necks so long?
*Their feet smell*!
**Charlene Cooper**

Why do the French eat snails?
*They don't like fast food*!
**Laura Thompson**

# SCHOOLY JOKES

Mum: What marks did you get in PE last term?
Small Girl: *I didn't get marks, I just got bruises*!
**Rebecca Bartlett**

Teacher: Where is Felixtowe?
Child: *On the end of Felix's foot*!
**Grant Norgrove**

Why did the teacher wear sunglasses?
*Because her pupils were so bright*!
**Claire Wilcockson**

Teacher: What do you call the outside of a tree?
Boy: *I don't know, Miss*
Teacher: Bark!
Boy: *OK, WOOFF*!
**Saninder Virdee**

What insects shy away from school?
*Tru-ants*!
**Ben Witcher**

Teacher: How far are you from the correct answer?
Child: *two seats, Miss*!
**Philip Bartlett**

Teacher: Why do birds fly south in the winter?
Boy: *It's too far to walk!*
**Charlotte Zeki**

Teacher: Your story about 'My Dog' is exactly the same, word for word, as your brother's.
Boy: *I know, Miss, it's the same dog!*
**Rebecca Bartlett**

Teacher: Jim, if you had £12.50 and you asked your gran for another £2, how much would you have?

Jim: *£12.50, Miss.*

Teacher: That's not right, you don't know how to add.

Jim: *And you don't know my gran, Miss!*

**Jenny Lacock**

Teacher: What's your name?

Boy: *Henry.*

Teacher: Say, Sir, Henry

Boy: *OK, Sir Henry.*

**Grant Norgrove**

Teacher: I've changed my mind.

Cheeky boy: *Does the new one work any better?*

Teacher: If you had £1.90 in one pocket, and £4.67 in the other, what would you have, Fred?

Fred: *Someone else's trousers on, Miss!*

**William Trimble**

Teacher: Is this your brother?
Boy: *Yes, Sir*.
Teacher: He's very small.
Boy: *Well, he's only my half brother*!
**Grant Norgrove**

# THANKS TO THESE SCHOOLS FOR PROVIDING THE JOKES!

Alcott Hall Junior School, Solihull
Blackwood JMI School, Sutton Coldfield
Cranford Park Primary School, Harlington
Cutteslowe First School, Oxford
Harris Middle School, Lowestoft
Landulph County Primary School, Saltash
Leverets School, Stow on the Wold
Midfield Primary School, Orpington
Model Primary School, Ballymoney,
Northern Ireland
Moorfields Primary, Ballymena,
Northern Ireland
Parkhill Junior, Ilford
Roscoe Junior School, Liverpool
Southbury Primary School, Enfield
St George's School, Windsor
St William of York School, Bolton
Tannaghmore Primary School, Lurgan,
Northern Ireland
Taupaki School, New Zealand
Thurlbear CE Primary School, Taunton
Tower Hill Primary, Witney
Whitehall Primary School, Bristol
Withington County Primary, Hereford

Wood Green School, Witney
Woodlands Park Junior School, London
Wycliffe CE Middle School, Shipley

# What's black and white and read all over?

So said David Parfitt of Earby County School, Earby, Lancashire.

But David will have left this school long ago, because the original *Schoolkids' Joke Book* was published in 1987! The jokes, however, will continue to delight for years to come because they were all collected, playground fresh, from schools in Britain (and forces schools in Germany) by Books for Students, the school paperback bookshop specialists. Edited by Brough Girling, there are hot favourites, old chestnuts, crispy new jokes – something for everyone. If you've enjoyed *The Schoolkids' Joke Book Too!* you'll love *The Schoolkids' Joke Book*.

## And there's another lost diary waiting to be discovered...

# THE LOST DIARY OF ERIK BLOODAXE, VIKING WARRIOR

## VIKING SCANDAL – GORBLIME TELLS ALL!

Newly discovered diaries and logbook cuttings reveal that famous Viking king, Erik Bloodaxe, couldn't write. However, his court poet Gorblime could and he gives astonishing details of life in Viking times.

- Battles and butchery
- Longships and love
- Births, marriages and plenty of deaths
- Poems and prisoners
- Erik's victories and his wife's vengeance
- Viking gods and Viking myths
- Travel and adventure

and much, much more.

# And there's another lost diary waiting to be discovered...

## THE LOST DIARY OF QUEEN VICTORIA'S UNDERMAID

### VICTORIAN SCANDAL – SCRUBBER TELLS ALL!

Newly discovered diaries reveal rather more than should be seen or heard of Queen Victoria! Astonishing details of Victorian life from above and below stairs, faithfully recorded by one of HMQ's faithful servants .

- Incredible inventions
- Passion and politics
- The Queen and her Empire
- Albert and efficiency

- Death, drains and duty
- Suds and sea-bathing
- War and work
- Exhibtions and excitement and much, much more

'we are not amused'

# Order Form

To order direct from the publishers, just make a list of
the titles you want and fill in the form below:

Name .................................................................................

Address .............................................................................

.........................................................................................

.........................................................................................

Send to: Dept 6, HarperCollins Publishers Ltd,
Westerhill Road, Bishopbriggs, Glasgow G64 2QT.

Please enclose a cheque or postal order to the value of
the cover price, plus:

UK & BFPO: Add £1.00 for the first book, and 25p per
copy for each additional book ordered.

Overseas and Eire: Add £2.95 service charge. Books will
be sent by surface mail but quotes for airmail despatch
will be given on request.

A 24-hour telephone ordering service is available to Visa
and Access card holders: 0141- 772 2281

Collins
An *Imprint* of HarperCollins*Publishers*